THIS BOOK IS ABOUT

_____

PREPARED WITH LOVE BY

_____

IN THE SAME SERIES, TWO BEAUTIFUL RECORD BOOKS.

A Mother Remembers. Written with love for my daughter.
Grandmother Remembers. Written with love for my grandchild.

OTHER GIFTBOOKS BY HELEN EXLEY

The Baby Blessing
Forever Your Baby Boy
Forever Your Baby Girl
Baby Boy!
Baby Girl!
Little Baby, Little Treasure
To someone special, celebrating your LOVELY NEW BABY
To a very special SISTER
To a very special BROTHER
To a very special MOTHER
To a very special DAD

Published in 2010 by Helen Exley Giftbooks in Great Britain. A copy of the CIP data is available from the British Library on request. All rights reserved. No part of this publication may be reproduced or transmitted in any form or by any means, electronic or mechanical, including photography, recording or any information storage and retrieval system without permission from the Publisher.
Printed in China.

Illustrations by Angela Kerr and words by Helen Exley, both © Helen Exley 2010.

12 11 10 9 8 7 6 5 4 3 2

ISBN: 978-1-84634-468-8

Published by Helen Exley®
Helen Exley Giftbooks, 16 Chalk Hill, Watford, WD19 4BG, UK.
www.helenexleygiftbooks.com

Baby
RECORD BOOK

BY HELEN EXLEY
ILLUSTRATED BY ANGELA KERR

A HELEN EXLEY GIFTBOOK

Introduction

Here is a journal that enables you to keep a record
of some of the most amazing and joyful experiences in life –
the first weeks and years of a child's existence!

Write down the events as they occur –
all those happy, chaotic and hilarious moments.
Then, later on, you will be able to focus
on this time in your life and relive it all with a smile.
Babies are babies for such a short time.
Enjoy it and remember to record everything.
Glue in lots of photographs and your child's first drawings,
and rewrite headings so that they're relevant to you.

This book will make a precious memento
for both you and your child – and perhaps, one day,
even for your grandchildren.

Helen Exley

Contents

The birth	8
First visitors	9
What your arrival meant to us	10
Family tree	11
Important relatives and family friends	12
Some family history	13
About Your Mother – and a message for you	14
About Your Father – and a message for you	16
Your Grandparents – a little of their lives	18
Messages from your Grandparents	19
Our home – your room	20
The world as it was when you were born	21
Firsts in the early months	22
Funny moments	23
Mementos	24
Things to remember	26
Outings	28
Growth chart	30
Your best-loved things in your first year	32
Medical records, immunizations	34
One very special day	35
Celebrations, Festivals, Parties, Fun!	36
Our family	38
Milestones	39
First sounds and words	40
One year old	42
After one year – your most-loved things	44
A typical day	46
Milestones as you grew	48
The worst times	49
Talents and interests as you grew	50
Early drawings	52
Early writings	54
Your early hopes and ambitions	56
Important events of your childhood	57
Things you said	58
Things we'll always remember	59
My letter to you now that I have met you…	60

The Birth

PLACE

DATE TIME

WEIGHT LENGTH

WHAT YOU LOOKED LIKE

THINGS WE WILL NEVER FORGET

A SPACE FOR A PHOTOGRAPH

First visitors

A SPACE FOR CARDS, MEMENTOS OR A PHOTOGRAPH

WHAT THEY SAID ABOUT YOU

MESSAGES, GIFTS AND FLOWERS

what your arrival meant to us

Family Tree

GREAT GRANDPARENTS

GREAT GRANDPARENTS

GRANDPARENTS

AUNTS AND UNCLES

PARENTS

BROTHERS AND SISTERS   BROTHERS AND SISTERS

YOU

Important relatives and family friends

A SPACE FOR A PHOTOGRAPH

Some family history

WHO THEY WERE AND WHAT THEY SAID

HOW YOUR PARENTS MET

About Your Mother

HER EARLY LIFE

HOW YOUR COMING CHANGED HER LIFE

HER DREAMS AND HOPES FOR YOU

A SPACE FOR A PHOTOGRAPH OF YOUR MOTHER

A message from your Mother

About Your Father

SOMETHING ABOUT HIS LIFE BEFORE YOU CAME

WHAT YOUR COMING MEANT TO HIM

WHAT HE HOPES FOR YOU

A message from your Father

A SPACE FOR A PHOTOGRAPH OF YOUR FATHER

Your Grandparents - a little of their lives

A SPACE FOR A PHOTOGRAPH OF YOUR GRANDPARENTS

Messages from your Grandparents

Our home - your room

The world when you were born

PRESS CLIPPINGS INSTEAD OF PHOTOGRAPHS COULD BE ADDED HERE

Firsts in the early months

A SPACE FOR EARLY PHOTOGRAPHS

GRASPED A FINGER

HELD HEAD UP

RECOGNIZED A PARENT'S VOICE

RECOGNIZED YOUR OWN NAME

SMILED

DISCOVERED YOUR OWN HANDS

SUCKED YOUR THUMB

ATE SOLID FOOD

Funny moments

A SPACE FOR A PHOTOGRAPH OR MEMENTO

Mementos

| A LOCK OF HAIR | YOUR FOOTPRINT | YOUR HANDPRINT |

THINGS TO REMEMBER

Important health facts and records

Things to remember

Outings

PLACES YOU WENT

FIRST VISITS TO RELATIVES, THE SEA, THE FOREST, THE FAIRGROUND

Special days

PLACES AND THINGS THAT DELIGHTED YOU

TIMES WHEN IT ALL WENT WRONG

Growth chart

AGE	HEIGHT	WEIGHT
ONE WEEK		
ONE MONTH		
TWO MONTHS		
THREE MONTHS		
SIX MONTHS		
ONE YEAR		
EIGHTEEN MONTHS		
TWO YEARS		
THREE YEARS		
FOUR YEARS		
FIVE YEARS		

Significant points as you grew

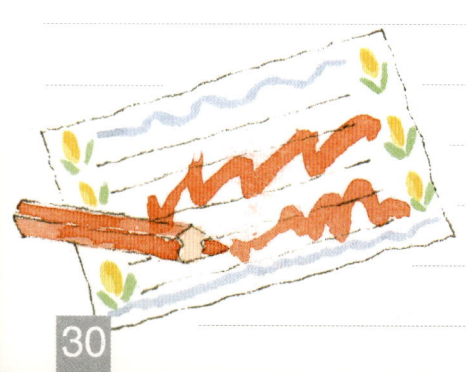

Tooth chart

1ST TOOTH	11TH TOOTH
2ND TOOTH	12TH TOOTH
3RD TOOTH	13TH TOOTH
4TH TOOTH	14TH TOOTH
5TH TOOTH	15TH TOOTH
6TH TOOTH	16TH TOOTH
7TH TOOTH	17TH TOOTH
8TH TOOTH	18TH TOOTH
9TH TOOTH	19TH TOOTH
10TH TOOTH	20TH TOOTH

UPPER

LEFT   RIGHT

A CHILD WILL HAVE 20 TEETH – YOU CAN RECORD AND LABEL WHEN EACH OF THESE TEETH APPEARS.

LOWER

Your best-loved things

PEOPLE, SONGS, TOYS, RHYMES, MUSIC – ANYTHING AND EVERYTHING

SPACE FOR A LITTLE MEMENTO

SPACE FOR A LITTLE MEMENTO

Medical records

DOCTOR'S VISITS	DATE
ILLNESSES	

ALLERGIES

BLOOD GROUP

OTHER IMPORTANT INFORMATION (FAMILY HEREDITARY DISEASES)

Very important! Keep accurate details for future reference

IMMUNIZATIONS	DATE

One very special day

FOR A CHRISTENING OR NAMING DAY, OR AN IMPORTANT HAPPY DAY FOR THE FAMILY

SPACE FOR ONE OR TWO SPECIAL PICTURES

Celebrations! Festivals! Parties! Fun

SPACE FOR ONE OR TWO PHOTOGRAPHS

Our family

TRADITIONS. WHAT WE ARE LIKE. WHAT WE DO. WHAT WE ENJOY.

Milestones

FIRST LAUGHED OUT LOUD

FIRST WAVED BYE-BYE

FIRST RECOGNIZED YOURSELF IN THE MIRROR

FIRST PRESS-UP

FIRST ROLLED OVER

FIRST CRAWLED

FIRST SAT UP UNSUPPORTED

OTHER IMPORTANT FIRSTS

First Sounds and words

RECORDING THE DATES COULD BE IMPORTANT, TOO

SPACE FOR MEMENTOS

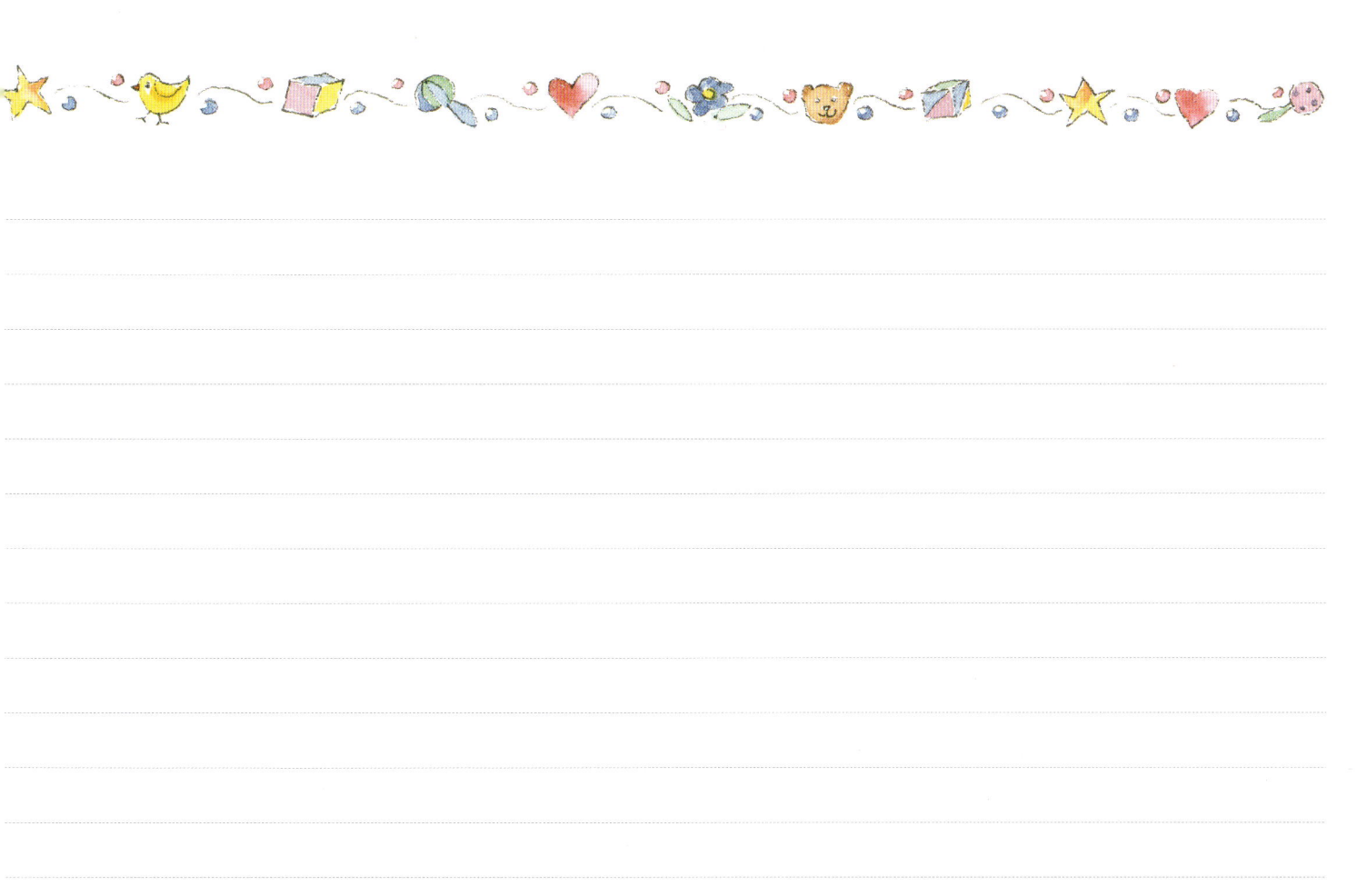

One year old

SPACE FOR A PHOTOGRAPH

After one year – the things you most loved

STORIES, SONGS, GAMES, FRIENDS

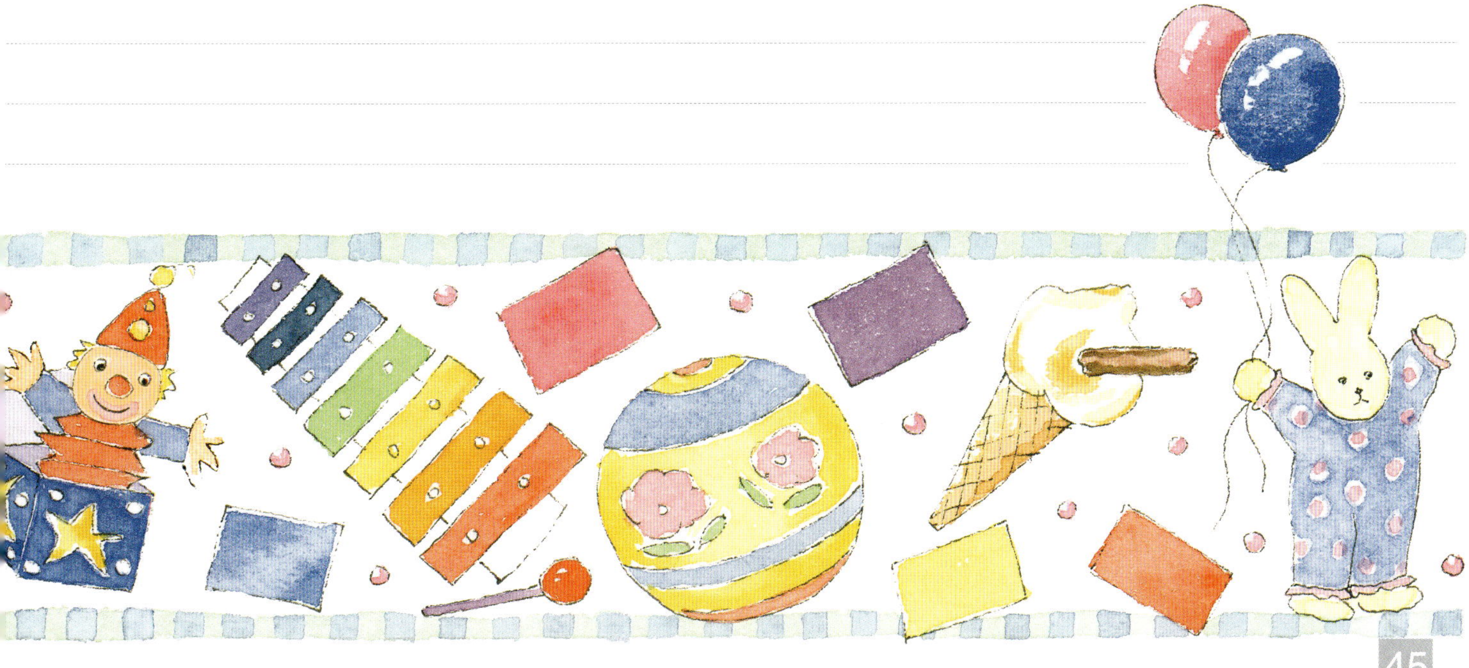

A typical day

AND LITTLE THINGS WE LOVED DOING TOGETHER

SPACE FOR A PHOTOGRAPH

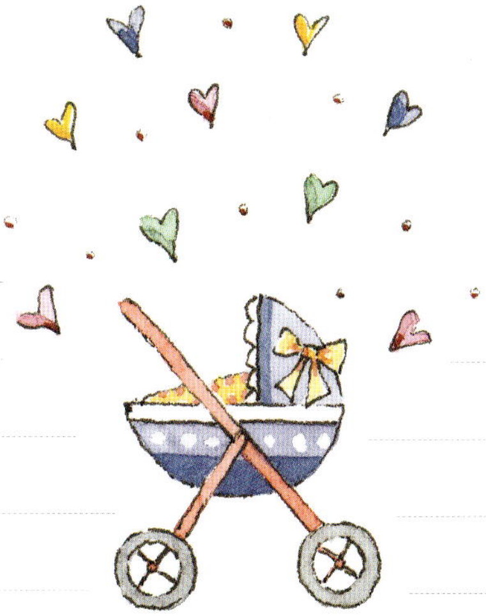

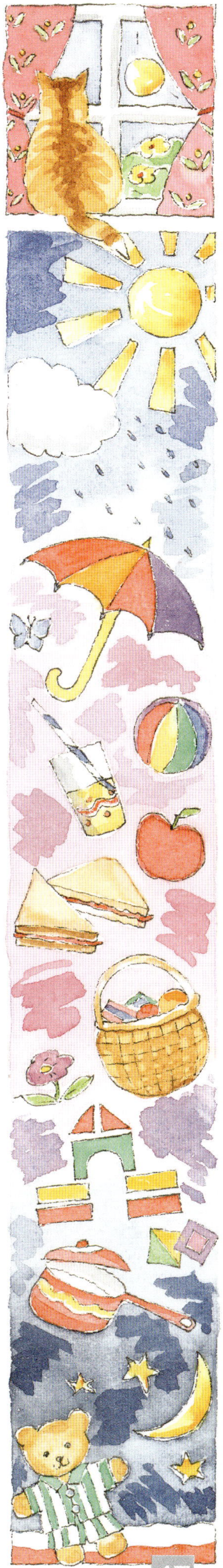

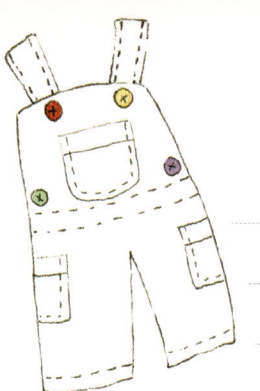

Milestones as you grew

SPACE FOR A PHOTOGRAPH

The worst times

THINGS THAT FRIGHTENED YOU

THINGS YOU HATED

ACCIDENTS AND DISASTERS

SAD EVENTS

YOUR FIRST MISCHIEF – AND PUNISHMENT

Talents and interests as you grew

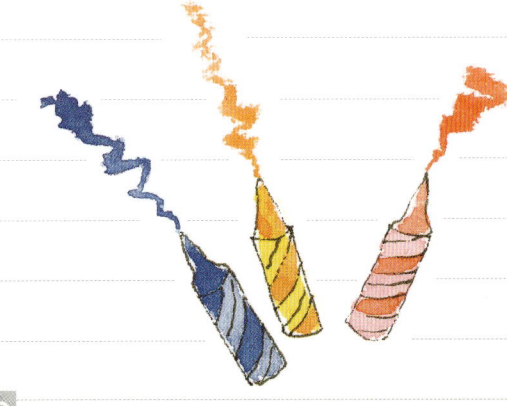

Early drawings

GLUE SOME EXAMPLES HERE

Early writings or squiggles

GLUE IN SOME EARLY EXAMPLES

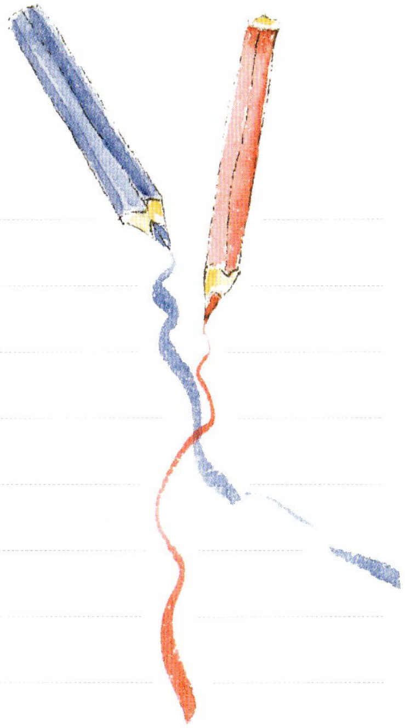

Your early hopes and ambitions

EARLY GOALS AND DREAMS

ACHIEVEMENTS

DIFFICULTIES YOU OVERCAME

Important events of your childhood

IMPORTANT THINGS THAT HAPPENED AS YOU GREW

Things you said

ALL SMALL CHILDREN COME OUT WITH DELIGHTFUL OR OUTRAGEOUS THINGS

Things we'll always remember

PARENTS, GRANDPARENTS AND PEOPLE WHO LOVE YOU COULD WRITE MEMORIES AND MESSAGES HERE

My letter to you now that I have met you...

Notes, photographs, mementos...